Devotions
by kids
like you

TAKE MY WORD FOR IT

INGRID
SHELTON

DAVID C. COOK
PUBLISHING CO.

Chariot Books™ is an imprint of David C. Cook Publishing Co.
David C. Cook Publishing Co., Elgin, Illinois 60120
David C. Cook Publishing Co., Weston, Ontario
Nova Distribution Ltd., Torquay, England

TAKE MY WORD FOR IT: DEVOTIONS BY KIDS LIKE YOU
©1992 by Ingrid Shelton.

Cover design by Rick Schroeppel
Cover illustration by Ken Coffelt
First Printing, 1992
Printed in the United States of America
96 95 94 93   5 4 3 2

Unless indicated otherwise, Scripture quotations are from the Holy Bible,
New International Version, © 1973, 1978, 1984, International Bible
Society. Used by permission of Zondervan Bible Publishers.

Verses marked TLB are taken from The Living Bible, © 1971, Tyndale
House Publishers, Wheaton, IL 60189. Used by permission.

Library of Congress Cataloging-in-Publication Data
Take my word for it: devotions / by kids like you; [compiled by] Ingrid
Shelton.
   p.   cm.
   "Chariot books."
   ISBN 1-55513-907-8
   1. Teenagers—Prayer-books and devotions—English. I. Shelton,
Ingrid.
BV4850.T35   1992
242'.63—dc20   91-32856
                                                CIP

Contents

About This Book

The stories in this book are true. They are told by teenagers like you who know what it is like to feel lonely or scared or depressed or full of questions. They've had to face divorce in their families, the suicide of a friend, the illness of someone they love, rejection by their classmates.

These teens all learned to trust God in difficult circumstances and found help by believing the promises in His Word. I asked them to share what was happening in their lives and how God has made a difference to them. As you read about their spiritual struggles and triumphs, your own faith will grow, and you will begin to see God working in your life too.

It is my prayer that God will use these stories to help you want to spend time with Him each day and to assure you that He is interested in every area of your life. As you learn to trust Him in all circumstances, you will be able to say with the psalmist, "But as for me, I will always have hope; I will praise you more and more. My mouth will tell of your righteousness, of your salvation all day long" (Psalm 71:14, 15a).

Content in New Jersey

My father is an electrician who works on construction. When work is slow in areas close to home, he goes where the work is.

About four years ago he went to New Jersey to work. Our family kept praying that a job would turn up near home, but it didn't happen.

During the summers we would leave our home and friends to be with my dad in New Jersey. At first I enjoyed it, but as I grew older it became boring. I kept thinking of all I could be doing with my friends back at home in Greencastle, Pennsylvania, where we could have picnics and slumber parties.

The third summer I was very unhappy, especially since there were no girls my age where we stayed. Then my parents decided that the family should not be apart any longer. We would all move into our travel trailer and live in a campground in New Jersey for the coming school year, and my mom would home-school us.

I was devastated. It looked like it would be forever before I could resume normal activities at home.

My mom knew I was unhappy when we made the temporary move to New Jersey. She asked me to review several Bible verses I had memorized before, and one of them was

5

Philippians 4:11, "Not that I speak in respect of want: for I have learned, in whatsoever state I am, therewith to be content" (KJV).

Now that verse began to mean something to me. As I slowly began to apply it to my situation in New Jersey, I learned there were other ways I could be content and happy.

Mom made arrangements for me to help in a nursing home where I enjoyed making friends with older folks. The campground owner also took an interest in us. He would take my brothers, sister, and me to look for deer, and he told us stories about different experiences in his life. I also found that there are some benefits to home schooling that I had never realized before.

When I learned the meaning of Philippians 4:11—being content anywhere—God chose to bless us.

After eight months in New Jersey, we moved back home to Pennsylvania, and my dad found a job only seven miles from our house. This was more than we had asked for.

Now we are together as a family at home where we can raise animals and where I can enjoy friendships with girls my own age. I thank God for giving me that experience, though. It taught me that if I submit to God's will instead of my own desires, I can be happy wherever I am or whatever I am doing.

CHERI DEGRANGE, 16
GREENCASTLE, PENNSYLVANIA

Not that I speak in respect of want: for I have learned, in whatsoever state I am, therewith to be content.
PHILIPPIANS 4:11 (KJV)

The Trouble with Running

Running came naturally to me and I loved it. Even though I had a knee and a hip problem, I had run races for a long time and had been pretty successful.

One day at the beginning of my freshman year, my friend Darren called. "We need some more runners for our boys' cross-country team. How about joining?"

"Sure," I said half-heartedly. "I could try."

I had wanted to join the cross-country team after eighth grade and had meant to practice that summer, but somehow I had been too busy. Now I would really have to work hard, and I was determined to do my best.

My first practice run was difficult because I wasn't in shape. I almost fainted halfway through. It wasn't long, though, before I was doing so well that I made it into the top seven. There was a competitive spirit among our team members that kept us running. We constantly tried to beat each other and our own records.

One day last October during a race with another school, pain hit my knee and I almost collapsed.

"Oh, no," I moaned as I slowed down. "Not again. I've got to finish this race. I can't let my team down. They're depending on me." I pushed myself to finish.

Later that day I got the news. No running for several days. I had pulled both my calf muscles, probably as a result of my knee problem.

As day after day went by and I had to watch my teammates run, I felt worse. I felt like I had let them down, and I became angry at myself and at the world around me.

I had hoped to help my team to victory. Instead I was sitting out like a vegetable.

Then I realized I was wallowing in self-pity. I knew the Lord has a reason for everything, and I had to accept my situation. I realized I was just as important to Him as a person as I was as a team member. I determined to trust God no matter what, even if I never got back to running.

After only a week, though, I had improved enough to run in the Mt. Baker Invitational Race. I knew I couldn't run like I usually did, yet I wanted to do well. Then it came to me. Instead of plodding, I loped along and I lengthened my strides. That day I had my best time ever, and I was pleased. I was glad when our team won second place, and we were able to go to the district races.

Now before races I pray for the Lord to give me strength and to help me do my best. Even during races, when I feel myself getting tired, I pray for God's help to finish. God helps me do my best.

DAN RUITER, 14
LYNDEN, WASHINGTON

. . . Let us throw off everything that hinders and the sin that so easily entangles, and let us run with perseverance the race marked out for us.
HEBREWS 12:1

Separated, but Together

Since my parents' divorce eight years ago, I have cherished the times I can spend with my father. He is in the Air Force and moves around a lot, but I always look forward to visiting him.

When I started thinking about Thanksgiving last year, I had a strong desire to see my dad. I called him on a dreary Sunday afternoon, and he seemed pleased that I wanted to come. We made plans for him to drive down and get me on a Tuesday, even though he lived four hundred and fifty miles away. Flying was out; neither one of us had the money.

I hung up the phone feeling excited and pleased. In less than three weeks I'd be with my father.

The time dragged on, but finally the weekend before Thanksgiving came. Saturday morning I woke up thinking "only three more days." At breakfast the phone rang. As I gingerly picked it up, a shadow of apprehension crossed my mind. Sure enough, it was Dad. His car had broken down, and he wondered if I could take the bus.

"No problem," I said, relieved that things would still work out. "It just means a shorter vacation."

Then my father called again. He would be leaving Wednesday for some base in South

Dakota. They needed him desperately because he was the best man for the job. That was the Air Force. I had known Dad could always be sent any place at any time. Before he hung up, he told me he would miss me, he was really sorry, and he still loved me a bunch.

I cried myself to sleep that night, and in the morning I woke up feeling depressed and gloomy.

I pulled out my Bible and devotion book. The reading for the day was called "The Most of Your Time." It was about finding the will of God and then making your plans. The Bible reference was Proverbs 16:3: "Commit to the Lord whatever you do, and your plans will succeed." I had never once thought to ask God if such a trip was in His plan for me.

I really missed not being with my father that Thanksgiving, but I accepted it and kept trusting God to work it out for good. Over Thanksgiving I spent valuable time with other people in my family. I felt good about it, and it was fun.

I know disappointments will come in life, but I also realize that God knows what's best for me and I can always trust Him.

MICHELLE KAMPSTRA, 16
MENO, OKLAHOMA

Commit to the Lord whatever you do,
and your plans will succeed.
PROVERBS 16:3

No Longer Embarrassed

When I was three years old, my dad, a high school music teacher, attended a band masters convention in Brookings, South Dakota.

The rest of our family went along to visit my grandparents in Elkon.

We were traveling home on a cold, dark night in February. When we got into the car, I told my dad to buckle his seat belt because Big Bird said everybody should. Unfortunately, Dad didn't listen.

Soon my brother Greg and I were asleep in the back seat. The next thing I knew I was sitting on a man's lap in an ambulance.

Two girls who were driving home from a drug and alcohol party had hit our car head-on. The girl who was driving blacked out and her car swerved into our lane.

Dad turned the wheels straight for the ditch, but not fast enough. Because he wasn't wearing a seat belt, he hit the dashboard and was knocked out.

For three weeks Dad lay unconscious in the hospital. Seven months later he came home with brain damage caused by the blow to his head.

Twelve years have passed since the accident. Although my dad's condition has improved, he is still like a child. He can't remember things that just happened, and he has to be helped to do basic things. His actions often embarrass me. At church he says "Amen" at the most inappropriate times. I often don't want my friends to see him.

But slowly I have learned to accept my dad. I realize he can't help what happened or the way he is.

I see how God is using him to minister at the Christian school where my mother teaches and my brothers and I attend. Dad is really an encouragement to everyone.

I've also learned to accept other handicapped people and classmates who maybe aren't as popular. God's command to love one another includes everyone. I know that if I don't love others who are different from me, I will miss out on blessings God has for me through them.

RENEE MOTTER, 15
MILLER, SOUTH DAKOTA

Dear friends, let us love one another, for love comes from God. Everyone who loves has been born of God and knows God. Whoever does not love does not know God, because God is love.

I JOHN 4:7, 8

My Friend Tonya

I noticed Tonya right at the beginning of my ninth-grade school year. She seemed like the kind of person who would appreciate Christianity.

Sometimes after school or at lunch we'd talk, and from our conversations I realized that Tonya wasn't a Christian and didn't go to church.

Slowly I got to know her better. One day I told her how I had become a Christian and what Jesus meant to me.

"Are you a Christian, Tonya?" I asked.

"No, I'm not," she answered thoughtfully.

I prayed a lot for a few weeks. I felt a responsibility to reach Tonya for Christ, but I knew I had to rely on God to work in her life. I invited her to our church youth group that met every Tuesday night for Bible study.

"I'd love to come," Tonya said without hesitation. "But I can't this Tuesday. Maybe another time."

I was glad Tonya was interested in coming, so I invited her again the next week and she came. Even though Tonya understood some things about the Lord, she was still confused about salvation. After the youth meeting she told me how much she had enjoyed it, and when I invited her back she quickly agreed.

As she kept coming back, week after week, she

began to understand that God loves and cares about her.

God isn't just some authority in the sky who wants to discipline everybody. Tonya learned that God is a friend who is always ready to help.

Usually after our Tuesday night youth group, my friends and I would go to the A & W for root beer. One Tuesday Tonya and I were walking to the restaurant together. I was still concerned about her relationship with the Lord, so I asked, "Did you ever ask Jesus Christ into your life?"

"Yes, I did," Tonya said sincerely. "It was after my third time at youth group that I realized I needed to ask Jesus to forgive me of my sins and to come into my life. At home I prayed about it. Now I know Jesus is my Savior and I'm sure of eternal life."

Today Tonya attends our youth group regularly, and she has started to come to church. She is reading her Bible and is excited about her relationship with God. I'm really happy that Tonya became a Christian, and I thank the Lord for helping me share my faith with and pray for her.

Curtis Harder, 14
Clearbrook, British Columbia

"I have made you known to them, and will continue to make you known in order that the love you have for me may be in them and that I myself may be in them."
John 17:26

I Promised Not to Tell

When Alisha's sister, Cindy, phoned to tell me that my friend was in the hospital, I froze.

I knew what she was going to say next before the words were out of her mouth.

"She tried to kill herself. The doctors said she would have died if Mom and Dad had arrived five minutes later," Cindy continued.

My stomach knotted and I crumpled to the floor. "How did she do it?" I whispered.

"Poison. She swallowed poison."

My hands began to shake so much I could hardly hold the phone.

Alisha and I had talked about suicide more than once. I had normal teenage problems. Boys. Jealousy. Boredom. Alisha was a Colombian adoptee. She felt stupid because she was sixteen and only in eighth grade.

We were sick of living. We wanted to escape. Sometimes when life got rough, we'd say that we wouldn't be back at school the next day, but we always were.

During the next few days I cried a lot, not out of sadness or regret, but out of confusion. I watched her family go through so much pain, and I blamed myself. A part of me wanted to tell, but I had sworn not to say anything.

Guilt, hatred, and destructiveness grew within me. I got some poison and hid it within reach. As time dragged on, I became a nervous wreck. I knew I couldn't take it much longer.

Although I had accepted Jesus as my personal Savior, I wasn't very close to Him. I still felt like such a sinner.

I wasn't certain I would go to heaven if I committed suicide. Death seemed so final, so dark.

One day I got up my courage and went to see Alisha's mom. "I knew Alisha was going to try to kill herself," I finally blurted out.

Alisha's mom took my hands in hers. I expected her to be angry, but she just held my hands, stroking them as if to reassure me. Suddenly the tears started pouring and with them my whole story.

"Marciana, do you still have the poison?"

I nodded.

"Will you promise me you will get rid of it?"

I hesitated, but when she asked again, I agreed.

"Will you promise to tell me or some other adult if you ever feel so bad you might kill yourself?"

I nodded, realizing I needed help with this.

Now, three months later, Alisha seems happy again. We don't talk about death anymore.

I know God has forgiven me and loves me no matter what. I also know that suicide is definitely NOT the answer. I know in this life I will have some problems, but I can trust God to work them out.

MARCIANA MEYER, 15
SEATTLE, WASHINGTON

So do not fear, for I am with you;
do not be dismayed, for I am your God.
I will strengthen you and help you;
I will uphold you with my righteous right hand.
ISAIAH 41:10

It Took a
Long Time

One day in 1982, missionaries came to our house to
share the Gospel with my family. We were Navajo
Indians who practiced traditional Navajo ceremonies.

My mom invited them into the house, and
they talked about how God sent Jesus to die on
the cross for us. They told us that by confessing
our sins and asking Jesus into our lives, we could
be sure of eternal life.

My family didn't care about their message and
were glad when they finally left. Yet something of
what they said stayed with us. As God said in His
Word, "So is my word that goes out from my
mouth: It will not return to me empty, but will
accomplish what I desire and achieve the
purpose for which I sent it" (Isaiah 55:11).

**Life went on as usual after that. My parents, who were
addicted to alcohol, continued to drink. Then about two
years later, my dad was put in jail.**

I didn't think anything good would come of
that, but one day when we visited him in jail, he
told us he had accepted Christ as his Savior. We
were surprised.

Later my mom came to know Jesus as her
Savior too. Now every time we visited Dad, Mom
and Dad would pray together. I couldn't
understand it. I wondered if God really did exist.

When my dad was released from jail a few months later, I could see a change in my parents. They prayed to the Lord. They didn't drink anymore. They no longer practiced traditional ceremonies.

We began attending church, and I didn't like it. Life wouldn't be fun anymore, I thought.

About a year later, one of my older sisters accepted Christ as her Savior. This was hard for me because we were very close and had done a lot of things together. Now she was changed. I knew God was speaking to me about giving my life to Christ too, but I wasn't ready.

When I was fourteen years old, we had camp meetings at church. As I listened to God's Word I knew I no longer wanted to live without Christ, so I gave my life to Jesus.

Most of my family are Christians now, but four of my brothers are still struggling with alcoholism. We pray for them and believe God will save them at His perfect time.

I've learned that God doesn't always answer our prayers right away. I thank the Lord for what He has done in my life and for what He is going to do.

CORRINA CHIQUITO, 16
COUNSELOR, NEW MEXICO

So is my word that goes out from my mouth:
It will not return to me empty,
but will accomplish what I desire
and achieve the purpose for which I sent it.
ISAIAH 55:11

The Wrong School

From first grade through ninth, I went to a Christian
school and loved it. Then the bottom of my world
dropped out.

The cost of my Christian school was too high,
and my mom said I'd have to transfer to the
public school.

"Why, God?" I screamed silently. "Please,
don't let this happen."

I don't have a father, so I have had extra
opportunities to learn to depend on God. In the
past I have seen God do many miracles, such as
provide money anonymously in our mail slot on
the day we'd spent our last penny. I knew God
could do it again, so I sent up urgent prayers,
begging Him to provide the money somehow.

**Finally, after several weeks, I came to the point where I
could tell God "not my will, but yours be done." I was
ready to accept whatever God had for me, and both my
mom and I had a real peace about it.**

That summer my mom registered me for tenth
grade at the public school, taking along some of
my report cards. When the secretary saw my
grades, she mentioned that I might fit into the
school's challenge program. But, she told my
mom, I'd have to wait a year since the testing
had already been done the previous March.

My mom went to talk to the people in charge of the program. They just happened to have one open space for tenth grade, and because they were testing another student the next day, I was allowed to take the exam as well. I was accepted!

I know all this didn't just "happen." I am sure God wanted me in that public school, for in the challenge program I am happier than I have ever been in school. (I've never worked so hard, either!)

I know there is another reason I am in the public school at this time. I met a girl there I hadn't seen since kindergarten. We have become good friends, and I am praying and trusting God that she will become a Christian soon.

Today I praise the Lord for working it all out. God has proven a better Father than I could ever have on earth. He truly knows what I need and will never leave me short.

TANYA WEBER, 15
VICTORIA, BRITISH COLUMBIA

A father to the fatherless, a defender of widows,
is God in his holy dwelling.

PSALM 68:5

Locked in a Hospital

I have schizophrenia. Or at least I had it.

I'm not sure how my mental disorder started, but slowly I became more depressed, lonely, and unhappy, and finally my life didn't seem worth living.

After several attempts at suicide, I was admitted to a mental hospital in Utah. In the hospital, away from my family and friends and church, where the doors were always locked and where even my personal belongings were taken away from me, I became even more depressed.

I wasn't sure about my relationship with the Lord. I believed in God, but I was not a committed Christian. I'd pray sometimes, but I felt I wasn't getting through to God.

I often wanted to die. Many times I cut my wrist; I felt so depressed. Other times I heard voices in my mind that were telling me to kill myself.

All this time I was on some medication that was supposed to help me, and for a while it seemed that the drugs did help. A few weeks later I was sent home, but not for long. When I again attempted suicide, I ended up back in the hospital. I knew my family and friends were disappointed, but I just couldn't help myself.

Often my pastor came to visit. At first I was embarrassed, especially when he prayed in front of my new friends in the hospital. One day my pastor told me that the church had been praying that God would take away my depression and silence the voices in my mind. He gave me Philippians 4:13, "I can do everything through him who gives me strength." He told me that God could give me the will to live and help me live a happy life. Before he left, we prayed together.

I kept thinking about that Bible verse, and I realized how much I needed God. That day I recommitted my life to Christ.

I knew I needed God's help every day, every hour. I couldn't get out of the hospital on my own. With God's help I could desire not only to live, but also to live a Christian life.

When I had gone for seventeen days without cutting myself—the longest time in four years—I was well enough to go home. I was determined to overcome my mental disorder completely and to trust God to constantly fill my mind with His love.

Today I am no longer depressed, because I know Jesus lives in my heart and I have made Him Lord of my life. Even though it looked almost hopeless, God answered my prayer and He is healing my mind. I am glad that nothing is impossible with the Lord.

JACQUI WARNER, 16
SANDY, UTAH

I can do everything through him who gives me strength.

PHILIPPIANS 4:13

The Record Player

That was it. My record player had had it. I'd owned it for six years, but now it wouldn't last another day.

"I just have to get a new record player," I told myself as I put away my favorite record. Right away I went to the nearest Radio Shack to see what they had to offer. As I looked around, I found one I liked, but it cost $95.00. All I had in my pocket was one dollar and a few cents.

The more I thought about that record player, the more I felt sure it was the one for me. But how could I buy it? Even if I saved up my allowance, it would take about a year.

I decided to pray about it.

Six weeks later I received a hundred dollars for my birthday!

I was surprised and happy and sure that God answered my prayer. I'd saved my allowance, and even if I gave 10 percent of my birthday money for tithe, I could still buy that record player.

The next day I returned to the store, but when I looked at "my" record player, I was surprised. The sale was over and the cost was now $112.99. Even with my savings, all I had was $104.00. I couldn't buy that record player after all . . . or could I? If I didn't tithe, then it could be mine today.

Hadn't the Lord answered my prayer and provided the money for it? Maybe I just shouldn't tithe this time.

Then I remembered what I had read in the Bible a few days earlier: "Will a man rob God? Yet you rob me. But you ask, 'How do we rob you?' In tithes and offerings" (Malachi 3:8).

I knew I could not buy the record player. God had to come first.

Just then the store clerk came over. "Shall I pack it up for you?" he asked, when he saw me looking at it again.

"No," I answered. "Sorry. I only have a hundred and four dollars."

"I think I can let you have it for that, including tax," the clerk said.

Later, when I was unpacking my new record player at home, I was thankful to the Lord for working out this problem. I was glad I had decided to obey God's Word and give Him the money I owed.

God has given me so much. It is only right that I return to Him a part of what I receive.

THORSTEN BRAUN, 13
WESTON, ONTARIO

But seek first his kingdom and his righteousness, and all these things will be given to you as well.
MATTHEW 6:33

The Diet

It started as a simple diet. Everyone goes on diets—I'd been on many already.

It was January, the heart of winter, and I was carrying some extra pounds that I'd put on at Christmas. Now I wanted to lose every inch of fat, because our youth group was going to Thailand in March for two weeks. Although our purpose was to visit refugee camps, I knew we would also have some fun times on the beach, and I wanted to look good in a bathing suit. So I began to cut down on food and spend most of my free time exercising.

Being thin became the most important thing in my life. Doing exercises before bed replaced my quiet time with God.

If I prayed, it was for more discipline to exercise and for forgiveness for breaking my diet.

Things got worse. Thoughts of food would come into my mind as I was praying, and I would have to stop and eat. Then I would feel guilty and work it right off.

When I left for Thailand I had reached my weight goal, but I still felt fat. I didn't see how anyone could like me. While in Thailand, I couldn't stop eating.

When I came home, I had a hard time trying to stop. I didn't like going out in public where everyone could see that I had gained weight.

I knew I was sick, and I hated myself. I blamed God and everyone else around me for what was happening.

Finally I realized I was caught in a destructive cycle and I needed help. I realized that my focus was wrong. I was sinning against God by not loving myself, His creation. I needed to change my whole attitude and love myself the way God loves me, with an accepting and forgiving love.

As I began to put God first and spend time in His Word, He began to bless my efforts of exercising. The more I filled myself with the food of His Word, the less I felt the urge to eat. Psalm 119:103 became my motto: "How sweet are your words to my taste, sweeter than honey to my mouth!" When the enemy put thoughts of food in my mind or gave me a negative attitude about myself while I was praying, I claimed God's promises of strength to overcome.

It's a struggle sometimes, but each day I must yield to God's Spirit and His leading so He can use me for His glory. Today I don't crave food the way I did before. With God's help I can control my eating disorder and accept myself the way I am.

God had to teach me a hard lesson, but I'm glad He did. I know as I seek God first, everything else will work out all right, including my eating habits.

JENNIFER SHELTON, 16
VANCOUVER, BRITISH COLUMBIA

So whether you eat or drink or whatever you do, do it all for the glory of God.
I CORINTHIANS 10:31

A Father Who Understands

Life was perfect when I was five. I had a little sister and a great mom and dad who spent a lot of time with me. I also had two sets of grandparents nearby who always welcomed a visit from their only grandson.

One Saturday night just before I started kindergarten, I spent the night at Grandma's house. As I snuggled into my sleeping bag, little did I know that life as I knew it would be shattered.

My dad, a policeman, left for work as usual. That night he was shot in the head and died. It was such a shock to all of us. I could hardly believe that someone would kill an innocent person like my dad.

We spent the next three years trying to rebuild our lives. My grandpas were especially helpful. They gave Mom advice and acted as dad to my sister and me, but just as we began to adjust to being a threesome, Mom married again.

Unfortunately, that marriage didn't work out the way we had thought it would. First, we had to move from Iowa to Minnesota. We left our family, friends, and church. In addition, I had to leave the only house I had ever lived in. And worst of all, Mom and my new dad fought a lot.

I was lonely and frustrated. When I had a problem or just wanted to let off steam, I couldn't call my

grandparents as I had before. Sometimes I felt like running away. I wanted to go to live with my grandparents, but I knew Mom would bring me back.

When I thought of my mom and stepdad always fighting, I could barely stand it. I felt more miserable and lonely than ever. Many times I talked to God about it. Would things ever change?

Then at the end of my sixth-grade year, my mom, sister, and I packed up and returned home to Iowa. A divorce followed. Somehow I felt relieved after these changes, and life seemed better. I could again call my grandparents for advice and comfort, and the church became even more important to me, though I still felt a bitterness toward my stepdad.

I really had to pray about this because I knew the Lord didn't want me to be bitter. As I kept on praying and trusting God more, the Lord took that bitterness away.

There was no way I could have made it without the Lord. He was the One who comforted me during periods of extreme loneliness.

Now I can understand others who go through similar experiences, and I can comfort them. I can tell them that God is there for us always and our heavenly Father always understands and cares.

TODD J. HILL, 16
DES MOINES, IOWA

Praise be to the God and Father of our Lord Jesus Christ, the Father of compassion and the God of all comfort, who comforts us in all our troubles, so that we can comfort those in any trouble with the comfort we ourselves have received from God.
II CORINTHIANS 1:3, 4

Not to
Sri Lanka!

When my dad received a phone call from a close friend asking if our family would possibly be interested in going overseas as short-term missionaries, I was stunned. The whole idea sounded dreadful.

Missionaries? Not us. Weren't missionaries the unstylish and out-of-it type of people? I could not picture myself out in the middle of the jungle with none of the necessities that I, a normal teenage girl, would need.

"Why us, God?" I prayed selfishly. "Don't You care about my well-being?"

Yet after my parents' earnest prayers, the Lord saw fit to send us for a year as missionaries to Colombo, Sri Lanka, a small island off of India.

As I stepped off the plane in Colombo, I thought I could actually see the heat floating by as I felt the sweat pour off me. Yet the culture shock was still to come.

The people were really different. The guys were not too tall and just about skin and bones. The ladies had yards and yards of clothes wrapped around their bodies and earrings stuck through their noses. Some were dark and others light colored. Most of them wore no shoes or just worn-out slippers.

At first we found the roads impossible to drive on because they were so crowded. Anything and everything was on them, including taxis, vans, buses, cows, horses, elephants, bicycles, motorcycles, cars, and people. As long as our car horn worked, we were fine. Also, all vehicles drove on the left-hand side of the road, which we found difficult to get used to.

The scenery was breathtaking though. There was so much greenery. The palm trees of Sri Lanka were quite a change from the pine trees of Nebraska!

The first two weeks seemed almost unbearable, and I was ready to go back to the States. My mom came down with dengue fever, a relative of malaria, and we all suffered with fevers, chills, severe bone aches, rashes, and depression.

Life did seem to improve, though, and I actually began to like it there. I attended an international school with more than five hundred students representing forty nationalities. At our church I met some really neat Sri Lankan teenagers and learned more about their culture through teens' eyes.

A year later when our term was up, I realized that God must love me and care about me very much to give me such a new experience.

God opened my eyes to the extreme need for the Word of God to be spread to other people and to how important that task is.

LYNN HOTZ, 15
RUSHVILLE, NEBRASKA

And my God will meet all your needs according to his glorious riches in Christ Jesus.

PHILIPPIANS 4:19

Grandpa's Grief

One day I answered the phone and heard my grandfather's voice.

"Jenny, is your mother at home?" he asked. His voice was trembling.

"No," I answered. "She just left for work."

"Okay," he said, then hung up quickly. I could feel in my spirit that something was wrong.

I had stayed home from school that day because I hadn't been feeling well. Now I sat back in the big armchair and wondered about Grandpa. I thought of the many times our family had prayed for him, yet he still wasn't a Christian. Grandma had been a Christian for a long time, and she prayed for him too.

About two hours later Mom called from work. "Grandma died of a massive stroke while she was asleep last night," she told me with tears in her voice. "At least she had no pain before death."

I was shocked. I had never experienced the death of someone close to our family.

Then I thought of poor Grandpa. How was he taking it? Grandma had been his life. I was afraid for him.

After I got ready, Mom picked me up and took me to Grandpa's house. I hurt when I saw

Grandpa slumped over. He was so sad he couldn't even speak.

At the funeral our pastor preached the best sermon I'd ever heard. He said that my grandmother was now with Jesus, in a place where there was no pain and no tears, but joy and peace. Someday we would see her again. Then he explained the way to God.

Grandpa cried right through the sermon. At the end we all bowed our heads, and the pastor asked those people who wanted to become Christians to raise their hands. Grandpa raised his. He was finally ready to ask Jesus into his heart and life.

We were all happy in spite of the sad occasion. It took a tragedy to bring Grandpa to Christ, but Grandma's life had pointed him to God. Something good had come out of Grandma's death, something good for eternity, and I was thankful for that.

JENNY SIDNER, 15
COLUMBUS, OHIO

Be strong and take heart,
all you who hope in the Lord.

PSALM 31:24

A Different Color

I was nine years old when Mom said she had to talk to me about something important.

"You know that you were adopted when you were two years old," she started. "We heard you needed a home, so we prayed about it and felt that God wanted us to be your parents. But what we've never told you is that you are biracial."

"Biracial?" I asked in amazement. "You mean, half white and half black?"

"Yes." Mom nodded.

I sat there a moment, too amazed for words. "Who are my real parents? And why did they give me away?"

"That's a long story," Mom said. She told me that I was born in Georgia when my birth mother was only sixteen years old and unmarried. My birth mother asked her own parents to raise me, because she felt she could not handle the responsibilities that came with a baby. My grandparents had agreed to take me, fully intending to raise me themselves, but certain circumstances developed that made it impossible for them to keep me. They loved me very much and asked an agency to find a good Christian family to adopt and love me.

"Who is my father?" I asked slowly.

"All we know is that your mother was white and your father black," Mom said.

So that's why I am brown, I thought. I had always known that my skin color was different from the rest of my family, but I had never understood why.

For a few days I could hardly think of anything else. I resented the fact that my mother had given me away as if I were a dog or a cat. Though I never had any contempt for black people, I hated that I was half black and half white. Why had God allowed this to happen to me?

Then year by year, God began to heal my hurt. I thought of how different my life would have been if I had not been adopted, and I began to count my blessings.

God gave me a Christian home. My father is the pastor of a Baptist church, and I accepted Christ as my personal Savior when I was nine.

I realized that what God said in Romans 8:28, "and we know that all things work together for good to them that love God, to them who are the called according to His purpose," (KJV) is true. I knew God had a purpose for my life and a reason for allowing this to have happened to me.

Today I am thankful for my Christian family. The Lord has helped me overcome some of the hurt I have because of my past.

The biggest goal I have is to return to Georgia and witness to my grandparents and my mother, and see them accept Christ as their Savior too.

MICHELLE BOERSMA, 15
BUCHANAN, MICHIGAN

The Spirit himself testifies with our spirit that we are God's children.

ROMANS 8:16

Friends Who Care

Denise's cozy house was warm and smelled of peach potpourri when she, Ashley, Trisha, and I came in the door sometime after nine o'clock that evening.

We were talking about our relationship with the Lord. At least, my friends were—I didn't say anything because I wasn't sure I was a Christian.

We were going to spend the night at Denise's, so we made ourselves comfortable, got some chips, popcorn, candy, and crackers, and began to watch a movie on video. Trisha soon fell asleep on the couch, but Denise, Ashley, and I were still up, eating and talking.

I kept wondering about my relationship with Jesus. I had gone to a Christian school since third grade and to church for about a year, yet I didn't know how I could be sure I was a Christian.

Finally I got enough courage to say, "I don't know if I really have a relationship with the Lord."

Denise and Ashley looked at me for a moment, surprised. "That's okay. We'll tell you how you can know," they said. "Let's go to the family room and we'll explain it to you."

We sat down on the couch and they told me all about what was going to happen in the future, how the Lord had helped them, and how great and powerful He is. "And when you have a problem and really need a friend, God will always be there," they assured me.

They also shared Bible verses with me that they knew, such as John 3:16: "For God so loved the world that he gave his one and only Son, that whoever believes in him shall not perish but have eternal life."

Then we joined hands and prayed, and I asked the Lord into my life. Ashley and Denise were so happy for me. They hugged me, and I thanked them for the new wonderful friend they had brought me to know.

Now I felt clean, like all my sins were washed away and a tremendous weight had been lifted off my shoulders. I was happy to finally know for sure that I was a Christian, and that when I died I would be with Jesus forever.

Today I trust and love the Lord with all my heart. I know He cares for me. Jesus is my best friend, and He will always be there with me. I'm praying that if any teens don't know Jesus as their Savior, they will find a teacher, parent, or friend like I did, and get to know the Lord better.

AMY FINN, 13
WHITTIER, CALIFORNIA

If we confess our sins, he is faithful and just and will forgive us our sins and purify us from all unrighteousness.

I JOHN 1:9

Too Busy

The wind rushed by me, picking up dead leaves, as I walked heavily toward my house. The strap of my schoolbag, which was full of homework I had been putting off, sank deep into my shoulder.

Resentment grew within me as I realized how much work I was facing: a math test the following day, two major projects due the next week, a book report, and a composition.

I'd barely started my homework when my mother called the family to dinner. *Why does she have to call us just now?* I thought angrily. The anger stayed with me as I began studying for the math test. I wrestled until eight o'clock with percents and interest concepts, and finally won.

Just then my younger sister came to me. "Your favorite show is starting. Watch with me?"

"No. I have too much homework to do," I informed her, determined not to get sidetracked.

She settled down to watch the show by herself, but I soon got caught up in the story. Before I knew it, I was making myself comfortable on the couch and stuffing my face with potato chips and dip.

After the show I worked madly on my report and outlined ideas for my project. I finally fell asleep at my desk around eleven-thirty. A little later I woke up and put myself to bed.

The next morning I slept in, and I had to rush to get ready for school. Then my eyes fell on my little white Bible lying on my dresser. Everything seemed to slow down. I picked it up and began to read.

I tried to recall whether I had remembered to pray the night before, as I usually do at night. I hadn't, but I also realized that if I had, it wouldn't have made a difference.

Prayer had become just a habit with me. A lot of things in my life had become a habit.

Right then I bowed my head and prayed like I hadn't prayed in a long time. "Dear Lord, thank You for stopping me today and showing me what I've missed. Please forgive me for being unfaithful to You after all You have done for me, for thinking I can do things on my own. I need You to guide me, to show me the way. I want to follow You in everything."

Things were different from that day on, especially my homework and prayer habits.

Now I pray each day for God's wisdom and direction. I realized I could no longer just "say a prayer," but must really spend time with the Lord, talk to Him, and let Him guide me. I know God is faithful to me and I want to be faithful to Him.

SUSAN CHENG, 12
MISSISSAUGA, ONTARIO

But be sure to fear the Lord and serve him faithfully with all your heart; consider what great things he has done for you.
I SAMUEL 12:24

Forsaken by Friends

I walked home from school alone, fighting back tears. At lunchtime I'd had a silly quarrel with my three best friends over some gossip they'd heard, and they'd walked out on me.

Sandra, Shelby, Lana, and I had been friends since third grade and did everything together. Sandra and I were especially close, almost like sisters.

The next day at school they ignored me. I thought that since I was the only one in our group who went to church, maybe it was up to me to make things right. On the third day, when things were still the same, I called each of them and apologized. They each listened politely and mumbled, "That's okay," then hung up. Even Sandra.

I was crushed. I had no other friends. Whenever I saw them they either dodged or ignored me. I wished I could change schools or quit.

Mom tried to encourage me. "Jesus was lonely too. Even His disciples left Him at the end."

I nodded, remembering that Jesus had died alone on the cross for my sins. I then realized that I hadn't told any of my friends about Christ, and even worse, I rarely talked to Jesus myself and seldom opened my Bible.

The next Sunday at church I committed my life fully to the Lord. I knew Jesus would never leave me nor forsake me. He quickly became my best friend. I talked to Him every day, told Him everything, and read His Word. As the weeks went by, I could even smile at my former friends when I saw them at school.

About four weeks later, Sandra called. "I'm sorry I ignored you, Mary," she said. "I really feel bad, and you've been so nice about it. Can we still be friends?"

"Sure, Sandra. It's all right," I told her. "Would you like to come over?"

"Be right there!" she yelled into the phone.

A few minutes later she was at my door. After we had caught up on the news, I told her about my relationship with Jesus and how He had helped me.

"You sure are different now," Sandra remarked thoughtfully. "Lana and Shelby feel bad about ignoring you too, but I don't think they're ready to admit it."

That night I thanked the Lord for bringing Sandra back to me. Perhaps one day I would be able to share Jesus with Lana and Shelby, too.

MARY ANNE KLASSEN, 14
MATSQUI, BRITISH COLUMBIA

"Peace I leave with you; my peace I give you. I do not give to you as the world gives. Do not let your hearts be troubled and do not be afraid."

JOHN 14:27

Not Doris

When I first found out that Doris had cancer, I
totally denied it. She had been one of my best
friends for more than six years, and best friends
do not get cancer.

I met Doris when I was eight and moved from
Texas to South Dakota. I was shy and had difficulty
making new friends, but Doris was outgoing and
friendly. Soon we were best buddies.

Over the years our friendship grew. I could tell
her anything. Doris' mother was Mom number
two to me, and her older brother teased me
without mercy.

When five years later my dad, who is a pastor,
agreed to take a church in Kansas, I was
devastated. Doris's family offered to let me live
with them for the rest of the school year, but my
dad thought it was more important for the family
to stay together. Leaving Doris and my other
friends was the hardest thing I had ever done.

Then in March of 1988, Doris's father called
with some sad news. Doris had been diagnosed
with Hodgkin's disease, a kind of cancer that
affects the lymph nodes.

**"No! No! No!" I told God. "She's so full of radiance and
energy. Why did this happen? Why her, and not me?"**

Eventually God brought peace to my heart

concerning Doris's situation. I saw her a few times during that year, and although she seemed tired and paler, she was the same Doris I had always known. She went through chemotherapy and radiation, and later had a bone marrow transplant.

One day when Doris and I talked on the phone, we came up with the brilliant idea that maybe I could visit her at the hospital in Omaha. When my father attended meetings at Grace College of the Bible, I was able to go along.

Doris was weak and tired easily, but the cancer had not defeated her. Her beautiful personality was still there. God's strength was sustaining her.

One night I listened with admiration as Doris explained to her doctor how "all things work together for good to those who love God." I could see the doctor's respect for Doris as Doris continued to witness to her.

Doris is back home now and is doing well. In a testimony to her church recently, she said, "It doesn't matter whether I live or die. Either way I am the winner."

Doris continues to be an example to me. When I get weighed down by problems, I think of Doris and how she, with God's power, overcame one of the greatest problems life could bring her.

Kristi Reimer, 15
Newton, Kansas

Do not be anxious about anything, but in everything, by prayer and petition, with thanksgiving, present your requests to God. And the peace of God, which transcends all understanding, will guard your hearts and your minds in Christ Jesus.
Philippians 4:6, 7

Peace on a Miserable Night

It was a typical night in the hospital, a vacuum of silence. The only sounds were the quiet rhythmic tap of the night nurse's shoes in the long hall . . . and the sound of my crying.

Two days earlier the doctors had removed pieces of bone from my hip, whittled them into the shapes they needed, and transplanted them into both my feet in another reconstructive surgery to correct my club feet. What a bummer—twelve surgeries in ten years.

I couldn't sleep. My feet and hip felt like they were on fire, and I had an itchy rash from an allergic reaction to the codeine in my pain shots. With casts up to each knee and my feet propped up on a mountain of pillows, I was totally helpless. Besides feeling excruciating pain, I was also feeling exhausted from the long surgery. I was scared.

Self-defeating thoughts crowded into my mind. *Why me? Why couldn't I just be normal?* I was angry and upset. I had dreamed of becoming a surgeon, but how could I get through medical school and perform surgeries from a wheelchair?

During this surgery the doctors had built a new big toe on my right foot so that I would be able to walk without stumbling or falling. They had also removed bone from my left big toe and rearranged muscles and tendons so I could wear a normal closed-toe shoe on my left foot instead of just an open sandal.

How many times I had wished I could run, play basketball, and walk around enough to go shopping at the mall for a couple of hours.

Through my handicap, though, God has given me a lot of compassion and understanding for other disabled people. As I thought about all the irritations of being in a wheelchair, I also realized that because of my disability, I have met some wonderful people and have had some unique experiences.

Then I remembered my favorite and most comforting Scripture verse. "For I will give you peace, and you will go to sleep without fear" (Leviticus 26:6, TLB). My frustrated sobs stopped. It was as if Jesus were leaning over me, holding my hand and whispering.

I suddenly understood that when God promised to give me peace, I could, with His help and strength, cope with anything I had to face. Despite the day's restless hours, I was able to go right to sleep because I had accepted His promise.

TAVIA LIN GILBERT, 12
TWIN FALLS, IDAHO

For I will give you peace, and you will go to sleep without fear.

LEVITICUS 26:6A (TLB)

Through Crying Eyes

Elaine was witty, sensitive, and a nonconformist. She wore her hair spiked or shaved, powdered her face white, and lined her eyes in black. She was punk and she was tough.

She was bitter at the senseless stupidity of war, prejudice, murder, and political eras like the Holocaust. Even as a teenager she devoted her life to changing the evil in the world. Elaine, like so many other youth, never saw goodness, and mistakenly thought that in such an evil world God could not exist.

Since the October day I first met Elaine, I felt I had to pray for her. She was one of the most wonderful people I had ever met, and I wanted her to experience my joy in Christ.

One day Elaine became a victim of the evil she had fought against. The police found her body in a house in downtown Toronto, beaten, strangled, and burned. The people who so brutally murdered my friend were some drifters she had known for a long time.

"Why, God, why?" I screamed out in pain. "Why haven't You answered my urgent prayers? I've prayed for more than a year for her salvation."

That summer was a spiritual nightmare for me. No encouragement from my home or church helped. I

couldn't understand why God allowed this tragedy to happen.

I thought that sending Elaine to hell for not believing in Him was cruel. For months I was unable to open my Bible or pray. I wasn't sure I even believed in God anymore.

Then a cousin sent me a Bible verse from II Peter about Christ not wanting anyone to perish. After reading it, the verse "Jesus wept" (John 11:35) entered my mind. A few days later I heard a song about how through crying eyes God sees the sin and hatred in this corrupt world. I realized that God also suffers because of the sin and unbelief of the world. All these factors started me on the road toward emotional and spiritual healing.

I now understand that Jesus wanted Elaine to live. He hated the sin that killed her. Salvation was there for her throughout her life. Even while she was dying, Jesus held out His life to her from the cross.

God hadn't deserted her. He had sent me to pray for her and to love her. God hadn't deserted me either. He had given me privileged time to know Elaine and be touched by her life.

I still have many unanswered questions, but essentially I am at peace. I have been able to pick up my life and go on, knowing that God understands and cares. Although I still cry for Elaine, I am thankful today that my peace and joy are rooted in Christ.

LORETTE C. THIESSEN, 16
NIAGARA-ON-THE-LAKE, ONTARIO

He is patient with you, not wanting anyone to perish, but everyone to come to repentance.

II PETER 3:9B

The News

'll never forget that warm spring night when my mom told me the news.

I was sitting in the old wicker chair in her office, and she was sitting in the swivel chair in front of her computer. We were talking about the changes that would be coming into my life when I started junior high in September. Until we had that conversation, though, I didn't realize just how many changes there would be.

"Chris," she said, "I know you might be upset about this, but we've decided to put you in a Christian school next year."

I was more than upset. I was hurt and mad and scared.

I didn't want to go to some new school where I didn't know anyone. I'd heard about Christian schools too—they were tough and strict and mean. I knew I was going to hate it, but my parents made me promise to at least give it a try.

Before my mom dropped me off at school the first day, we both prayed that God would help me get used to the new school and make friends quickly.

I did a lot of silent praying too. Even though I had to admit the teachers and the kids at my new school were really nice, it took weeks of praying before I got rid of the butterflies in my stomach and began to feel like I really belonged.

I'm not sure exactly when it happened, but sometime during the school year I realized that I was looking forward to getting to school in the morning and seeing my friends. Our combined seventh and eighth grade class had fewer than twenty-five students, and we all got very close. We had a lot of fun together, and we supported and encouraged each other.

The teacher I had thought would be mean turned out to be a nice guy who really cared about us. Even the principal (commonly known among the students as "Godzilla") turned out to be a pretty nice lady (most of the time).

At the awards assembly at the end of the school year, I got some news again, only this time it was really good news. With all my new friends standing on the stage with me, I got the award for being the most improved boy student in the seventh grade.

That's when I knew that God had really answered my prayers about getting used to my new school and making new friends. I also realized that when I face changes in the future, God will always be there to help me.

CHRIS MILLS-HENDERSON, 13
SANTA PAULA, CALIFORNIA

God is our refuge and strength,
an ever-present help in trouble.

PSALM 46:1

My Search for Love

I need you, Mom. Please, show me that you care," I screamed silently as I found the bottle of pills I had hidden. I really didn't want to die, but I had to do something to get my mother's attention.

Mom and Dad, both alcoholics, divorced when I was in seventh grade. When Mom immediately brought home a new boyfriend, I was devastated. I still looked up to my dad. I hurt so much that I had tried to kill myself then, but a neighbor found me in time.

Things didn't get any better after that. Mom was away from home a lot, and I was left to baby-sit my two younger sisters, do the housework, and even cook. I wanted to have fun with my friends and not have all that responsibility.

When I was fifteen I moved into a friend's house, hoping that life would be better. Soon I realized that my friends were more of a problem than a solution.

The parties and drinking didn't make me happy. I missed my mom so much. If only she could see my loneliness and take it away.

I better get this over with before anyone comes home, I thought as I swallowed the handful of pills. As I became drowsy, loneliness and pain just overwhelmed me.

A few hours later I woke up in the hospital, dazed and miserable but still alive. Mom came to see me, but even trying to commit suicide didn't bring me the love I seemed to need.

A few days later my aunt, who lived three hundred miles away, called and invited me to live with her and her family. I was glad to get away from my hometown because I didn't want to face anyone, but one thing bothered me. My aunt's family were Christians and went to church. I would have to go with them. I knew about God, but I didn't think He cared about me.

On my first Sunday there, we all went to church. A youth evangelist was speaking, and as I listened it seemed he was talking directly to me. "God wants to be your Savior, your heavenly Father. Only He can take away the hurt in your life and give you joy and peace," he said.

As he continued to talk about Jesus, it all made perfect sense to me. I knew this was what I needed, and I went to the altar to give my life to Christ. That day the Lord forgave me all my sins and began to do a work in me.

Since that time about eight months ago, Jesus has filled my heart with love, and day by day He has taken away my pain. I finally have something to live for. Now I love my parents and accept my mom, trusting that Christ will work in her also.

JENNIFER PATTISON, 15
ABBOTSFORD, BRITISH COLUMBIA

My soul finds rest in God alone;
my salvation comes from him.
He alone is my rock and my salvation;
he is my fortress, I will never be shaken.
PSALM 62:1, 2

That Cool Guy

I saw him as soon as I arrived at my aunt and uncle's house. Chad was every girl's dream—dark hair and a gorgeous tan.

I couldn't believe my good fortune, especially when I found out he was spending the night with my cousin.

Later that evening I saw him take out his Bible. What a cool guy. I wondered, was he a Christian, too?

After a while Chad said good night and went down the hall to the bedroom he was sharing with my cousin.

The house was still, but I had a hard time going to sleep that night. A little later I saw a quiet figure coming down the dark hall. My heart skipped a beat.

Chad came over and squatted down beside me. Then he took my hand and started pressuring me to do some things I knew were wrong. I was shocked.

"No," I said, pulling my hand back.

He started laughing.

"Why would you do that?" I finally asked.

Now it was his turn to be surprised. "I, I don't know. Why wouldn't you do it?"

I looked straight at him and said, "I'm saving myself for my future husband. I don't want my husband to have messed with a lot of other girls and then want to marry me."

"That's a good answer," he said, and walked away. I thought that problem would now be settled, but it wasn't. The next day he came in while I was watching TV and started in again.

Now I was really upset. "Look. I'm not ready for that," I told him, emphasizing my reason.

I remembered hearing about a girl who was being ridiculed for being a virgin. I'll never forget the answer she gave to the girl who taunted her, "I can become like you any day. But you can never be like me."

I am thankful that God gave me the wisdom and the strength not to yield to temptation. I know that if I honor the Lord in all areas of my life, He will take care of any situation.

MICHELLE MELTON, 16
NORTH POLE, ALASKA

Do you not know that your body is a temple of the Holy Spirit, who is in you, whom you have received from God? You are not your own; you were bought at a price. Therefore honor God with your body.
I CORINTHIANS 6:19, 20

Prayer Meetings... at School?

About a dozen or more teens were sitting or standing around and talking when I walked into room 101 of our high school. It was a quarter to eight, Monday morning.

"I guess it's time to get started," announced Dave, our leader. "Any prayer requests? Any answers to prayer?"

"Yeah. I have a physics test today," Chris spoke up. "Please pray."

"And I have an English essay due," I added.

"Please pray for Linda. I would like her to come to know Jesus," Rachel said.

The prayer requests kept coming.

"I was able to talk to Chad about Christ," Dan told us. "Thanks for praying."

After a few minutes we broke up into groups to pray for each other and for our friends. When the bell rang fifteen minutes later, we headed for our first period classes with a new determination and courage to be witnesses for Christ.

It's all part of belonging to ACTS (Active Christian Teens in School). We meet every morning before classes for prayer and twice weekly at lunchtime for Bible study. We also plan extracurricular activities for school participation.

ACTS started about two years ago when the

youth pastor of my church encouraged our youth group to be witnesses for the Lord at school. "Plant your flag at school," he told us. "Let others know that you are Christians."

At the beginning of the previous school year, our student body president, who was a Christian, challenged us to meet together regularly for prayer at school.

Prayer meetings at school? The idea seemed strange to me at first. I thought prayer meetings belonged in a church, or maybe even in a Christian school, but in a public school? I thought about it and talked about it, and I realized that praying with other Christian kids at school would be a fantastic way to begin each day.

Our prayer meetings began with a group of about five teens. Gradually more and more kids started coming, even some new Christians, and the fellowship and answers to our prayers made our meetings exciting.

Now I look forward to our daily prayer meetings. I feel I'm not alone as a Christian in a public high school where most teens don't care about the Lord. I also realize that there are teens who are searching for God. They don't yet know that He is there for them to be their Savior and friend.

DEAN BLUNDELL, 15
ABBOTSFORD, BRITISH COLUMBIA

"Therefore I tell you, whatever you ask for in prayer, believe that you have received it, and it will be yours. And when you stand praying, if you hold anything against anyone, forgive him, so that your Father in heaven may forgive you your sins."
MARK 11:24, 25

Triumph in Tragedy

'll never forget Tuesday, November 15, 1988. It was the day I said goodbye to my friend Greg.

As I sat at his funeral service, my thoughts turned back to the cold facts on the front page of yesterday's newspaper: "Gregory Mark Eli, a fifteen-year-old Whittier Christian High School student, was shot to death Friday in his home in the affluent Friendly Hills residential area."

Sitting a few rows in front of me were Greg's parents and five older brothers, shaken with grief.

I heard the pastor give a gentle reprimand to all teenagers present to speak out against evils like guns, knives, and drugs. Then he challenged us to turn this tragedy into triumph by changing our attitudes and lifestyles. I felt his words were directed to me.

As I lay in bed that night, I thought of what it must have been like that Friday in Greg's bedroom. He was talking on the phone to a girl while his three friends admired a .38 caliber handgun.

I bet they felt cool and daring with a real gun on a carefree Friday night with no parents at home.

I pictured them laughing and joking. Then in my mind I heard the explosion of the gun, the boys screaming and running in panic. The girl on

55

the phone probably screamed, "What's wrong? What was that noise?"

I could imagine the shock and horror Greg's mother must have felt as she came home three hours later and found her son lying on the bed in a pool of blood. Panic, tears, phone calls, confusion.

The Monday after Greg's funeral, I dreaded going back to school. Our classmates walked like silent zombies from class to class. As I stared at Greg's empty seat in my classroom, the sick feeling returned.

What a senseless accident. Or was it totally senseless? Was there some eternal purpose in it? I considered this question, and wiping away my tears I wrote a letter to Greg's mom and dad.

Dear Dr. and Mrs. Eli,

I can't imagine the suffering and grief you and your family must be going through right now. My family and I have been constantly praying for you, and we have shed many tears.

Since last Monday at Whittier Christian High School, sixteen kids have come to know the Lord or have rededicated their lives to Him.

I know all this does not make your grief any less, but I thought it might encourage you to know some of the good that has resulted.

It had to be Greg, who out of all his group had his life together. We look at his empty seat now, and know we will never be the same because of that Friday night.

Sherri Langan, 15
Whittier, California

And we know that in all things God works for the good of those who love him, who have been called according to his purpose.

Romans 8:28

Would God Do a Miracle Today?

She may be crippled for life," the doctor told my mom and dad at my birth. Mom and Dad were devastated.**

My displaced hip, completely out of the socket, would require surgery and more than likely would leave me with a permanent limp.

As the days and weeks passed, it hurt Mom to watch me in my metal brace and see me lying in my crib like a robot. I couldn't turn myself over, sit up, or do any other simple achievement that a healthy baby girl should be able to do.

My parents had just recently become Christians. They loved the Lord and studied His Word. They wondered if God could still do miracles today as He did in Bible times. Was it practical for today? Whenever they read the Bible, hope rose within their hearts.

Finally they decided to give God and prayer a try. Every day they stood by my crib to lay hands on me and pray, trusting God for a miracle.

Month after month they continued to do this in trust and dependence on God, even though they could not see any improvement.

One day when my parents took me to the doctor again, he suggested that X-rays be taken. When the results came back, my parents received some shocking but wonderful news. The hip had somehow been put back into the socket! No trace of a displacement could be found. The doctors were amazed, especially since the last X-ray had shown the problem to be getting worse.

My mom and dad were excited and happy and told the doctor about their prayers for me. The doctor was skeptical; he admitted that maybe I would be able to walk, but he said I would always be slumped over and have a limp.

Today, fifteen years later, I have no trace whatsoever of any physical handicap. I never had an operation and I can run, walk, and play like any other teenager.

I'll always remember what the Lord did for me. How great is His mercy to us! I am thankful that God gave my parents the faith to keep on trusting, even when things looked hopeless. I know God answers prayer. Whether the problem is big or small, nothing is impossible with the Lord.

AMY OREBAUGH, 16
FORT WORTH, TEXAS

And the prayer offered in faith will make the sick person well; the Lord will raise him up.
JAMES 5:15A

Burn-out

One day in ninth grade, my best friend pulled out a cigarette and said, "Try one. It will give you a little buzz."

I knew my parents didn't want me to smoke, but I didn't care. I thought they were trying to keep me from "the pleasures of life," so I tried it. I began to smoke regularly.

About three months later, my friend suggested we have a little party. When my parents went on a short holiday, we hauled two cases of beer over to my place and drank it all—just the two of us.

My parents were not aware of what I was doing, but my bad attitude affected our relationship.

That summer we had more parties, and I always ended up feeling miserable. Then one day my dad caught me smoking. I blamed it on my friend. I was banned from associating with him.

Just before tenth grade I saw an old friend who became my buddy. We both tried to follow the Lord, but soon he drifted away. The following December, he was killed in a car accident.

At first I was stunned and hurt, then I turned bitter. I knew God was trying to tell me that none of us can be certain of life, yet I turned against the Lord, even blaming Him for that tragedy.

I met my former best friend again. This time

he introduced me to drugs. I decided to go all out for narcotics, even if it meant destroying myself. I wanted nothing to do with God and didn't want Him to use me in His plan. Soon the kids at school had labeled me a "burn-out."

A false rumor passed around the school about me. At that point I didn't have enough money to buy all the drugs I needed to give me a lift. I became depressed, and life was unbearable. I tried to end it all by hanging myself. Fortunately I didn't succeed.

That's when my parents sent me to live with my brother in Vancouver. While I was there, a youth group presented a musical at my brother's church. Three of the guys stayed with us.

I noticed these guys had fun just by themselves—they didn't need dope or alcohol to have a good time.

I realized I could be that way too. That night I asked the Lord to forgive me, and I rededicated my life to Christ. I quit drugs and drinking, and went home a different person. God brought a Christian friend into my life who encouraged me.

Today I am sorry I rebelled against God and my parents. Nothing good came out of going my own way. Drugs didn't do anything for me, except almost destroy my life. They are far more dangerous than I once thought.

I know now that true joy and peace come from fellowship with God. I don't need drugs, alcohol, or cigarettes anymore because Jesus fills all the empty spaces in my life with His love. His friendship will last right through eternity.

Curtis Kliewer, 16
Clearbrook, British Columbia

Therefore, if anyone is in Christ, he is a new creation; the old has gone, the new has come!
II Corinthians 5:17

My Missing Dad

Right from the beginning, my life was hard. I was born in Chicago to a seventeen-year-old girl and a nineteen-year-old boy.

At that time my mother was lonely and scared in a big city full of people. My father worked as a signmaker and didn't make much money. Most of what he got went to buy drugs and alcohol.

Even our move to West Virginia didn't stop my dad from drinking and taking drugs. He rarely worked, and many nights he didn't come home.

There were times my mother cried for hours, and often Dad would become so angry he was destructive.

My sister and brother were born, then my mom and dad divorced. After that we rarely saw or heard from my dad. Mom, who had quit high school to marry him, went back to school and became a registered nurse.

During that time my mom's sister took me to Sunday school where I asked Jesus into my life, yet I still carried my own burdens. I hadn't learned how to trust the Lord with all of my problems.

When I was ten years old, Mom became a Christian and started going to church where she met a man she later married.

I was upset and bitter. I didn't want a stepfather. I wanted my father back, no matter what had happened.

Then I found out my dad had been sent to prison. I became so hurt and depressed that I thought of committing suicide. There was no one I could turn to with my troubles.

Mom told me that God could help, but I refused to accept that. Yet slowly, as I kept going to church, my attitude changed. I realized God loved me regardless of circumstances, and I recommitted my life to the Lord. Still, the hurt and bitterness wouldn't go away.

One day in church my pastor said that God doesn't want us to carry our hurt around. The Lord wants to heal our lives and emotions and give us joy.

That night I prayed about my problems, and the Lord healed my heart and gave me a love for my stepfather.

God also gave me a bonus. My dad has committed his life to God and will be released from prison soon.

Today I thank God for helping me understand that I can always trust Him and that He is always there to help with every problem in my life.

CASEY ROMERO, 13
SCOTT DEPOT, WEST VIRGINIA

We are hard pressed on every side, but not crushed; perplexed, but not in despair; persecuted, but not abandoned; struck down, but not destroyed.
II CORINTHIANS 4:8, 9

Our Turn Now

The first time my grandma had to be rushed to the hospital with internal bleeding was Thanksgiving. God answered our prayers, and soon she came back home.

The following Fourth of July, we were all looking forward to seeing the fireworks in downtown Columbus. Our plans changed when Grandma had to be taken to the hospital again. That night we watched the fireworks from an emergency room window of the hospital.

We learned that Grandma would need an operation, which was set for July 12th, my birthday. So on my special day our whole family—Mom, Dad, my brother and I, and my aunt and uncle—were again in the waiting room of the hospital praying for her.

When we prayed I felt calm, knowing God was in control. Our family drew close together.

Grandma pulled through the operation and even seemed to improve. But then on October 13, the day before my dad's birthday, Grandma was again rushed to the hospital. The whole family gathered again in the waiting room to pray for her. We were glad when the call came saying she was alive.

Grandma was having breathing difficulties, so we weren't able to see her until almost midnight.

**When I walked into Grandma's hospital room that
night, I was in awe. She had every conceivable machine
hooked up to her body, but worst of all she was in pain.**

I left the hospital room five minutes later, and
so did most of my family. It seemed no one could
see her suffer like that. As I started to walk away,
though, I felt something pull me back to her
room. I had to be by my grandmother's side
when others couldn't. That's the way our family
was. We all filled in where others had a weakness.
Now was my time to be strong. I sat by her side
and tried to calm her.

Later her kidneys stopped working and she
was put on dialysis, a machine that cleaned out
her bloodstream. On that day my mother and I
stayed with her from early morning until late at
night. It was the last time we were able to
comfort her.

When the Lord took her home to be with Him
soon after, a Bible verse from Job came to me,
"The Lord gave and the Lord has taken away;
may the name of the Lord be praised."

**All her life Grandma had loved us, no matter what we
did. Now it was our turn to show her we loved her and
would do anything for her. I know that families are
special. They are to love and to care for each other.**

MARK SCHOLL, 15
COLUMBUS, OHIO

*"The Lord gave and the Lord has taken away;
may the name of the Lord be praised."*
JOB 1:21B